Life As ...

Life as a Navajo Code Talker in World War II

Kate Shoup

Cavendish Square
New York

Published in 2018 by Cavendish Square Publishing, LLC
243 5th Avenue, Suite 136, New York, NY 10016

First Edition

Library of Congress Cataloging-in-Publication Data

Names: Shoup, Kate, 1972- author.
Title: Life as a Navajo code talker in World War II / Kate Shoup.
Description: New York : Cavendish Square Publishing, 2018. |
Series: Life as ... | Includes index.
Identifiers: LCCN 2017024130 (print) | LCCN 2017025423 (ebook) |
ISBN 9781502630537 (E-book) | ISBN 9781502630513 (pbk.) |
ISBN 9781502630544 (6 pack) | ISBN 9781502630520 (library bound)
Subjects: LCSH: Navajo code talkers--Juvenile literature. |
World War, 1939-1945--Cryptography--Juvenile literature. |
World War, 1939-1945--Participation, Indian--Juvenile literature. |
Navajo language--Juvenile literature. | United States. Marine Corps--Indian troops--Juvenile literature.
Classification: LCC D810.C88 (ebook) | LCC D810.C88 S55 2018 (print) |
DDC 940.54/8673--dc23
LC record available at https://lccn.loc.gov/2017024130

Editorial Director: David McNamara
Editor: Kristen Susienka
Copy Editor: Rebecca Rohan
Associate Art Director: Amy Greenan
Designer: Lindsey Auten
Production Coordinator: Karol Szymczuk
Photo Research: J8 Media

The photographs in this book are used by permission and through the courtesy of: Cover, National Archives; p. 5, 18 Everett Collection Inc/Alamy Stock Photo; p. 6 Keystone/Getty Images; p. 8 Bettmann/Getty Images; p. 10, 20 © CORBIS/Corbis via Getty Images; p. 14 McCarthy's PhotoWorks/Shutterstock.com; p. 22 AP Photo/Joe Rosenthal, File; p. 24 AP Photo/Lenny Ignelzi; p. 26 MIKE THEILER/AFP/Getty Images

Printed in the United States of America

Contents

Introduction

Members of the Navajo Nation in the American Southwest played an important role in World War II. They created a code based on their own language. They then used this code to quickly **encode**, send, and **decode** secret messages. These messages helped US commanders coordinate troops and warn them of danger. The Navajo did this even though the US government had tried to destroy them and their language in the past.

The Navajo Code was impossible for the enemy to **decipher**. It was kept secret until 1968. It was only then that the Navajo who worked with the code got the honor they deserved.

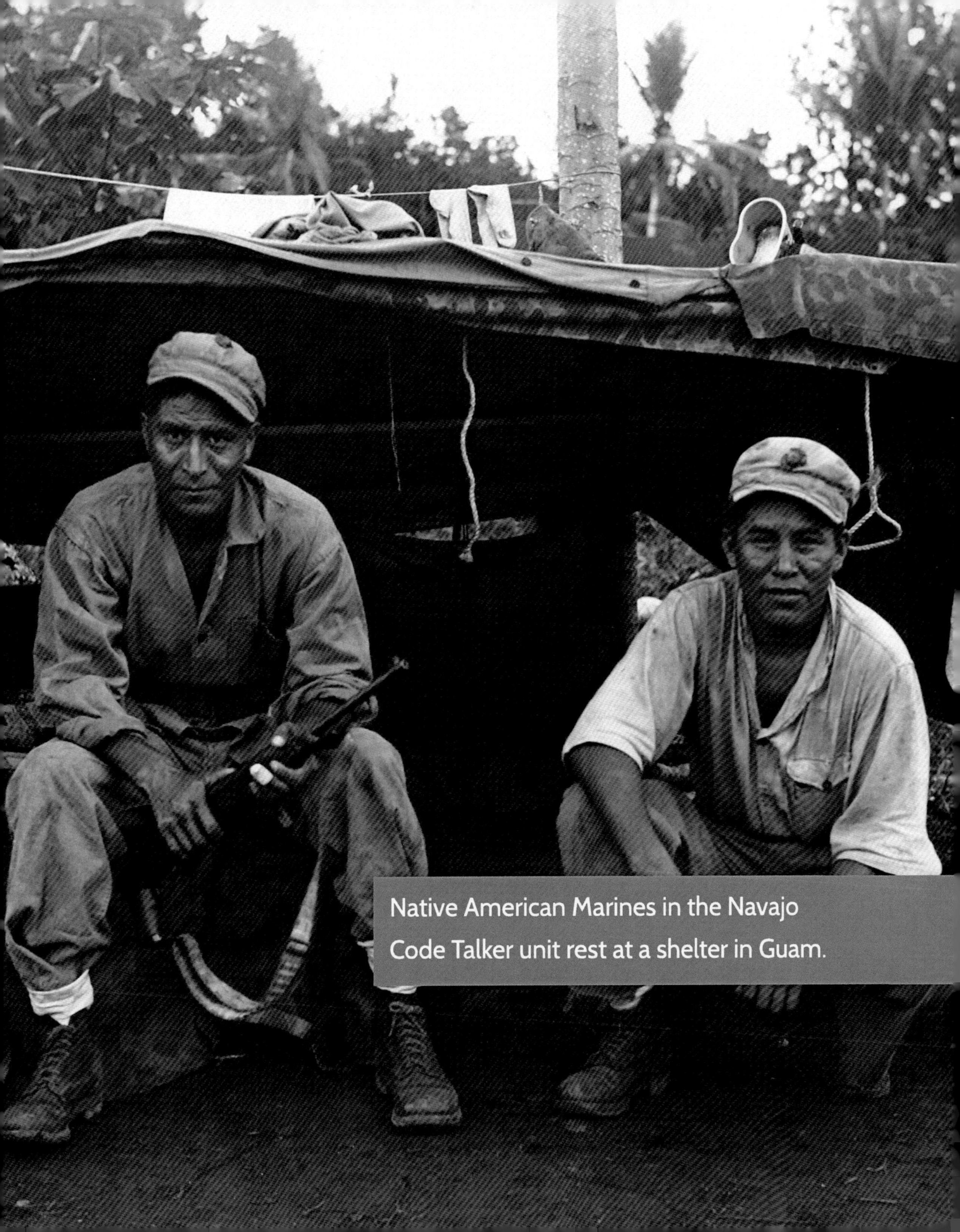

Native American Marines in the Navajo Code Talker unit rest at a shelter in Guam.

This infantry radio team works at a station in the Philippines in 1945.

Chapter 1

The Need for a Code

During World War II, American forces used codes to send messages to each other. This was so the enemy would not understand the messages. The soldiers used special machines to encode and decode the messages.

There were two problems with these codes. One was that the enemy often **cracked** the codes. This meant they could read the messages. Another was that it took American soldiers a long time to encode and decode the messages. This put military actions at risk.

In 1942, a man named Philip Johnston had an idea to solve these problems. His idea was to create a code based on the Navajo language.

Johnston thought the Navajo language would be a good code for three reasons. The first was that the

Many code talkers lived on the Navajo reservation before going to war.

The Two Sides of the War

World War II lasted from 1939 to 1945. In this war, Great Britain, France, the Soviet Union, and the United States joined forces. They were called the Allied Powers. Germany, Italy, and Japan were called the Axis Powers. Soldiers from the Allied Powers fought against soldiers from the Axis Powers in Europe and in the Pacific.

language is very complex. The second was that fewer than thirty people who were not part of the Navajo Nation could speak the language. The third was that the language had no alphabet. In other words, it was spoken but not written. This made it hard for outsiders to learn the language.

Code talkers often worked in pairs and were part of US Marine regiments.

Chapter 2

Code Talkers

Philip Johnston brought his idea to create a code based on the Navajo language to the United States Marine Corps. He showed that Navajos could encode, transmit, and decode a three-line message in just twenty seconds. The same message took thirty minutes using a code machine.

The Marine Corps was impressed. They recruited twenty-nine Navajo men who spoke both Navajo and English. These men created the Navajo Code. They wrote a dictionary for the code.

The Marine Corps recruited more Navajo men. Each one went through **boot camp**. For most recruits, boot camp was tough. For the Navajos, it was easy. They were used to hard work. During boot camp, recruits hiked for two days in the desert with only one **canteen** of water. Many of the recruits fainted from thirst. Not the Navajos. They squeezed water from plants to refill their canteens.

Other Code Talkers

Members of the Navajo Nation were not the only code talkers. There were also code talkers from other Native American tribes. There were Cherokee, Choctaw, Comanche, Lakota, and Meskwaki code talkers. There were also code talkers from Basque (part of Spain) and Wales.

After boot camp, these Navajo men were trained to use the Navajo Code. Many of these men were trained by Philip Johnston himself. They were called "code talkers" or "wind talkers." Each code talker learned the Navajo Code dictionary by heart. By the end of the war, there were around four hundred code talkers.

Philip Johnston

Philip Johnston was the son of a **missionary**. He grew up on a Navajo **reservation**. He often played with the Navajo children. He was one of only a few people who were not members of the tribe to learn to speak the Navajo language.

Code talkers traveled by ship to islands in the Pacific, where they fought the Japanese.

Chapter 3

The Life of a Code Talker

The US Marine Corps sent a few code talkers to Europe. These code talkers fought against German and Italian troops. However, most code talkers went to areas in the Pacific Ocean. These code talkers fought the Japanese.

The code talkers traveled by ship to different islands in the Pacific Ocean. They landed on Guadalcanal, Bougainville, Tarawa, Guam, Tinian, Cape Gloucester, Saipan, Peleliu, Iwo Jima, and Okinawa. These islands are very far away from the United States. It took a long time to reach them. The trip was not fun. It was hot, crowded, and smelly. The men slept on narrow bunks stacked four or five high. Food was scarce.

On each of these islands, the Americans fought the Japanese. These battles were very bloody. In the

Battle of Iwo Jima, almost seven thousand Americans and eighteen thousand Japanese died. In the Battle of Okinawa, more than twenty thousand Americans and as many as 110,000 Japanese died. In addition, hundreds of thousands of **civilians** were killed.

A Day for Code Talkers

For the code talkers, there was no such thing as a "normal day." Things were calm when the enemy was quiet. On those days, they might simply eat, rest, and make sure their radios were working properly. Things got more hectic when the enemy attacked. Code talkers transmitted and received messages about tactics and troop movements to commanders on the battlefield for hours during battle. They might not have time to eat or sleep. Each day was different, and each battle was a new challenge.

Code talkers were very important to the US war effort. They helped US forces coordinate during battle. They also warned US forces of enemy troop movements. This put them in great danger. The enemy tried hard to kill or catch code talkers.

The Marine Corps assigned bodyguards to the code talkers. These bodyguards went everywhere with the code talkers. Their job was to protect them. Thanks to these bodyguards, only six code talkers were killed by the enemy.

If a code talker was caught by the enemy, the bodyguard had a very different (and difficult) job: to kill the code talker. This was so the enemy could not torture the code talker to try to learn the code. Fortunately, no code talkers were ever captured.

Code talkers faced another danger. Their hair, skin, and features were similar to the Japanese. Sometimes, other Marines mistook them for the enemy.

Sometimes, Navajo code talkers worked for hours on end sending and receiving messages.

Chapter 4

Code Talker Tools

Code talkers used two main tools. One main tool was a radio. Code talkers used radios to send and receive messages. Each radio came with a headset, microphone, and antenna. Code talkers carried these radios in special backpacks. Sometimes code talkers used phones instead of radios.

The other main tool was the Navajo Code. The code was complex. First, the code matched English words to each letter in the alphabet. For example, one English word for the letter *B* was "bear." Another word for the letter *B* was "badger." A third word for the letter *B* was "barrel." Then, the code matched the English words with Navajo words. For example, the Navajo word for bear sounded like *shash*. The word for

Often, one code talker worked the radio while the other wrote down the message.

badger sounded like *na-hash-chid*. And the word for barrel sounded like *toish-jeh*. Code talkers spelled out messages using these "letters."

Certain words were not spelled out. Instead, they were translated directly into Navajo. For example, the Navajo word for jungle sounded like *woh-di-chil*. The word for kill sounded like *naz-tsaid*. And the word for warning sounded like *bilh-he-neh*.

Some English words could not be translated into Navajo. For example, there was no Navajo word for submarine. Instead, code talkers used the Navajo words for iron fish, which sounded like *besh-lo*. Similarly, code talkers called a fighter plane *da-ha-tih-hi*, or hummingbird, and they called a battleship *lo-tso*, or whale.

The other Marines respected the code talkers. One Marine said, "It was taken for granted they could interpret whatever we were transmitting."

US Marines raise the American flag on the island of Iwo Jima after winning an important battle there.

Code Talkers in Iwo Jima

Iwo Jima is an island in the Pacific Ocean. In the Battle of Iwo Jima, the Americans fought against the Japanese. There were six code talkers at this battle. During the fighting, the code talkers worked day and night. They sent and received more than eight hundred messages. They did not make a single mistake. Their commander at Iwo Jima was Major Howard Connor. After the battle, Major Connor said, "Were it not for the Navajos, the Marines would never have taken Iwo Jima."

Roy Hawthorne was a Navajo code talker.

Chapter 5

The Legacy of the Code Talkers

The Japanese cracked many codes used by the US Army and Army Air Corps. However, they never cracked the Navajo Code. This gave US forces an edge in the Pacific and helped them to win the war.

The Navajo Code was so strong the US government kept it **classified**. That meant the code talkers had to keep quiet about their part in the war. They could not even tell their families about their role in the Allied victory. That changed in 1968 when the US government revealed the code.

In 2001, President George W. Bush presented the Congressional Gold Medal to the original twenty-nine Navajo code talkers. Other code talkers received

Code talker John Brown Jr. (*left*) receives the Congressional Gold Medal of Honor from President George W. Bush (*right*) in 2001.

a Silver Medal. Both of these medals honored the code talkers. These medals are the highest awards US citizens can receive.

In 2008, the US government recognized other Native American code talkers, such as Choctaw code talkers, with the Code Talker Recognition Act. Code talkers and their tribes were celebrated at a special ceremony in 2013. At the ceremony, Senate Majority Leader Harry Reid said, "In this nation's hour of greatest need, Native American languages proved to have great value indeed. The United States government turned to a people and a language they had tried to eradicate."

Even though Native American communities had faced difficult times in the past, during World War II, each code talker took their responsibility seriously and performed courageous acts for their country. The code talkers will always have a special place in the history of World War II and the history of the United States.

Glossary

boot camp A training program for new military recruits.

canteen A special bottle in which to carry water.

civilian A person who is not in the military.

classified Describes a document or information that must be kept secret.

crack To discover how to read a code.

decipher Another word for decode.

decode To translate a message that was written as a code.

encode To make a message into a code.

missionary A person who moves to another area to try to get other people to join their religion.

reservation Land set aside for use by Native Americans.

Find Out More

Books

Hunter, Sara Hoagland. *The Unbreakable Code*. New York: Cooper Square Press, 2007.

Lewis, J. Patrick. *The Navajo Code Talkers*. Mankato, MN: The Creative Company, 2016.

Roesler, Jill. *Eyewitness to the Navajo Code Talkers*. Troy, MI: Momentum Books, 2016.

Website

Navajo Code

http://navajocodetalkers.org

Video

True Whispers: The Story of the Navajo Code Talkers

https://vimeo.com/188198031

Index

Page numbers in **boldface** are illustrations. Entries in **boldface** are glossary terms.

About the Author

Kate Shoup has written more than forty books and has edited hundreds more. When not working, Shoup loves to watch IndyCar racing, ski, read, and ride her motorcycle. She lives in Indianapolis, Indiana, with her husband, her daughter, and their dog. To learn more about Shoup and her work, visit http://www.kateshoup.com.